GEN Z

A 30-Day Devo Challenge Using a Made-Up Language for a Real Generation

IN PARTNERSHIP BETWEEN

SUNDAY COOL & STUFF YOU CAN USE

Published by Sunday Cool

The Word According to Gen Z: A 30-Day Devo Challenge Using a Made-Up Language for a Real Generation
Copyright © 2020 by Sunday Cool. All rights reserved.

No part of this work may be reproduced or transmitted in any form or by any means, electronic or mechanical, including photocopying and recording, or by any information storage or retrieval system, except as may be expressly permitted in writing by the publisher.

Dewey Decimal Classification Number: 242.2

Subject Heading:
DEVOTIONAL LITERATURE/BIBLE STUDY AND TEACHING/GOD

ISBN 978-0-578-75531-1

Scripture quotations are from the ESV® Bible (The Holy Bible, English Standard Version®), copyright © 2001 by Crossway Bibles, a publishing ministry of Good News Publishers. Used by permission. All rights reserved.

Printed in the United States of America

www.sundaycool.com

Table of Contents

The Authors	4
Introduction	5
How to Use	6

SECTION 1: THE REVERENCE OF GOD'S WORD

Day 1	8
Day 2	12
Day 3	16
Day 4	20
Day 5	24
Day 6	28
Day 7	32
Day 8	36
Day 9	40
Day 10	44

SECTION 2: THE MINISTRY OF THE WORD

Day 11	48
Day 12	52
Day 13	56
Day 14	60
Day 15	64
Day 16	68
Day 17	72
Day 18	76
Day 19	80
Day 20	84

SECTION 3: APPLYING GOD'S WORD

Day 21	88
Day 22	92
Day 23	96
Day 24	100
Day 25	104
Day 26	108
Day 27	112
Day 28	116
Day 29	120
Day 30	124
WHAT'S NEXT	128

The Authors

Carll Hooper is an enthusiastic, chicken-nugget-loving follower of Jesus who is the unofficial official spokesperson for *Sunday Cool Tees*. His videos have had millions of views, and are all created to benefit youth ministries across the globe. He is simply the best.

Brock Hooper is not only Carll's "too cool for school" cousin, but he's also the face of the Gen Z community. He's known for his supreme ability to translate modern day English into the Gen Z lingo and is surprisingly well versed in theology.

Andy DeNoon is a content coordinator for *Sunday Cool Tees* from Whitefish, MT. He currently lives in Mount Dora, Florida with his wife, Kelsey, and two children, Demi and Zola. He considers himself an expert on chicken wings, *The Office*, and has a passion for pursuing Jesus.

Josh Hooper is the content manager for *Sunday Cool Tees* and twin brother to Carll. He lives with his wife, Lily, in central Florida where he was born and raised. His passion is to share the gospel through any means necessary, using the platform God has given him.

Introduction

We're excited for you to be holding this devotional. Why? For one reason: it's all about God's Word. If you want to dive deeper, challenge yourself, and strengthen your relationship with the Scriptures while finding a little humor along the way, then this is the devotional for you. The book began with a video series we created that went viral in early 2019. The idea was simple: take the words in everyday life and Bible verses we have all heard before and translate them into funny and sometimes made up Gen Z lingo. Now, we are here taking the translations to another level and diving into the Word with a huge emphasis on just that: the Word. Over the next 30 days, you'll find three separate sections focusing on three pivotal parts of God's Word. The first is the reverence of God's Word. *Why should it be respected and held in high regard?* The second is the ministry of the Word. *How does Scripture meet us where we are and make us whole?* The final section will focus on application. *How do we take what we read and put it into action?* We are excited that you picked up this book because we know it's a great next step to discovering God through the devotion to and pursuit of His words.

A 30-DAY DEVO CHALLENGE

How to Use

We encourage you to approach each day the same way.

Before you begin each devo, ask God to show you something you haven't seen before. Ask Him to teach you a lesson you desperately need. Don't go into it with an agenda, low expectations, or preconceived notions. Approach the text with one purpose: to know God better.

Each day, you'll have one verse that goes with the section's theme translated into the Gen Z Version (our made up language). If it doesn't make sense to you, **don't worry. That's kind of the point.**

We will follow that up with the ESV translation, which is one of the best translations when it comes to being theologically precise and easy to read. **The Gen Z Version is the best for entertainment purposes.**

We would encourage everyone to have a physical Bible open when you go through the daily devo. None of the devos are super long, so make sure to read over each one well, taking in every word. Intentionally focus on what you're reading.

At the end of each devo, you'll find a list of biblical references we used to help write the devo or that we think will help you in your study. Feel free to read these to enhance your experience in the Word.

The following page will ask you to actually write out the daily verse in your own handwriting. We are more inclined to memorize what we write. And there is power in God's words. You can worship and honor God by writing out His Words.

Then we ask a few questions. Answer honestly and write whatever you feel you need to. **Don't hold back. Be real. Be honest.**

The final page includes what we want you to focus on for that day. We hope you can accept the challenge from each day, and take intentional steps toward applying the message to your everyday life.

On that page is an area for you to be creative. Use it for journaling, doodling, prayers, lists, or whatever you need.

At the bottom of each focus page, you'll find a QR code. Once you scan it with your phone, it will take you to a video made specifically for that day's devo.

This devotional is meant to strengthen the relationship you have with Jesus and His Word. So let's get started.

SECTION 1: THE REVERENCE OF GOD'S WORD

Day
ONE

GEN Z VERSION

Since Day Uno there was God. Jesus was chillin with God. And Jesus was God.

John 1:1

ESV TRANSLATION

In the beginning was the Word. The Word was with God and the word was God.
-John 1:1

HERE'S THE TEA.

It's tough to think about what happened before we were born. There was a time when people didn't have cars, electricity, TV, or YouTube. But it's even more difficult to think about what will happen when we die. We ask: *What will the world look like? Will people miss me? What about my family?* It can be tough to admit how small the part we play in this whole world really is. John shares that Jesus (the Word) was there before us. He had no beginning. He was there before the world was formed, and yet we feel Him missing in our lives at some of our lowest moments. We sense a hole in ourselves that we see as loneliness and seclusion. It can surround us and make us question, "Is God here? Does He even care?" The answer is *yes*. Sometimes we feel that hole because we aren't running after God. Sometimes it's because of trauma or hardships. But maybe God sometimes allows us to see that hole so we will realize how much we need Him and His words.

Focus on the enormous world God has created. Remember He values you and has since the beginning.

IF YOU WANT TO KNOW MORE
Gen. 1; Ps. 90:12; Prov. 16:9; Eccl. 3:11

1. Open your Bible and write out John 1:1.

2. What crosses your mind when you think of your time on earth?

3. Write down three words that come to mind when you start to realize how big God really is.

TODAY'S FOCUS:

Time

There's nothing wrong with catching up on your favorite show, but it is worth thinking about where we invest our time most consistently. If Jesus were living on earth today, how much Netflix do you think He would watch? How much time do you think He would spend on social media? How do you think Jesus would spend His time?

Challenge yourself today to focus on how you're spending your time. Keep track of it and evaluate it. How could you change your normal routine so you might make God's Word a constant focus throughout your day?

WATCH TODAY'S VIDEO

A 30-DAY DEVO CHALLENGE

SECTION 1

Day
TWO

GEN Z VERSION

God's wordz are one hundo, straight up slicing and dicin' and knowin' it all.

Hebrews 4:12

ESV TRANSLATION

For the word of God is living and active, sharper than any two-edged sword, piercing to the division of soul and of spirit, of joints and of marrow, and discerning the thoughts and intentions of the heart. -Hebrews 4:12

HERE'S THE TEA.

When you were a little kid, you were bound to fall and hurt yourself. And with that comes scratches and scars. Scars are reminders of a time when something pushed hard enough against you to physically tear you open and leave a mark. When a surgeon cuts into his patient, we know it will ultimately leave a scar. It will hurt, but we know the process is necessary for healing. God's Word is everywhere we look and is actively transforming even the hardest of hearts, leaving a lasting impact on those who have given themselves up to Him. Is God's Word truly active in your life? Is there evidence? God's words are so powerful that, if you let them, they can cut through to the deepest and most guarded parts of your character. We run to Jesus because, much like that surgeon, Jesus has the ability to save lives. But only Jesus can transform and save someone through His words alone.

Focus on how God's Word can pierce your heart and spirit.

IF YOU WANT TO KNOW MORE
Ps. 19:1-14; 2 Tim. 3:16-17

1. Open your Bible and write out Hebrews 4:12.

2. When you're reading the Bible, how open and vulnerable are you to allowing God to pierce your heart? Answer on a scale of 1 to 10, 1 being "not at all" and 10 being "completely." Explain why you chose that number.

3. Are there areas of your life that you wouldn't want God to change right now? Why or why not?

TODAY'S FOCUS:

Living and Active

If we could X-ray your heart, what do you think we would see? Would you be okay to see everything it contained?

God's Word cuts deep and has the ability to look into your heart, giving you the gift of discernment, faith, and so much more. So how will you open yourself up today to His Word? **Focus on allowing His Word to transform you today.**

WATCH TODAY'S VIDEO

SECTION 1

Day
THREE

GEN Z VERSION

I got your holy scripts padlocked in my chest thumper.

Psalm 119:11

ESV TRANSLATION

I have stored up your word in my heart, that I might not sin against you. -Psalm 119:11

HERE'S THE TEA.

Have you ever seen the safe at a bank? They are large and seem indestructible. If there is anywhere to keep valuable items, that would be the place. But think about how ridiculous it would be if you found out that, inside one of those massively secure safes, was something worthless. What if the safe held old clothes, bags of ramen noodles, or nothing but cheap furniture? Why would someone keep such useless items in a place so precious and secure? Well, this verse says David stored up God's Word in His heart. I'm no doctor, but I would say the heart is one of the most, if not *the* most, important parts of a person's body. So, if you were to store something inside, shouldn't it be valuable? Worthwhile? This is how we should see the words of God. His words are so holy that they deserve to be guarded in the most important place. If we fill our hearts with things of God, then our actions and thoughts will follow. We will leave less room for lies, bad habits, and selfish thoughts.

Be intentional about what you store up in your heart. Pay close attention to what you are prioritizing in your life right now.

IF YOU WANT TO KNOW MORE
Prov. 30:5-6; Matt. 6:19-21; 2 Tim. 3:16

1. Open your Bible and write out Psalm 119:11.

2. Take a look at your life. Where would you say the majority of your attention and interest lies?

3. List the top five most important things in your life right now, the first being the most important. Be honest. Where does God's Word fall?

TODAY'S FOCUS:

Store Up

Whether we realize it or not, we are all filling our hearts with either things of value or items that are worthless. Consider people you look up to and admire. What do you think they are focusing on in order to flourish and grow closer to Christ? **Choose one practical way to keep your focus on filling your heart with God's Word today.**

WATCH TODAY'S VIDEO

A 30-DAY DEVO CHALLENGE

SECTION 1

Day
FOUR

GEN Z VERSION

Not swerved by these scripts cause God be givin' that "get out of jail free" card to the whole fam.

Romans 1:16

ESV TRANSLATION

For I am not ashamed of the gospel, for it is the power of God for salvation to everyone who believes, to the Jew first and also to the Greek. -Romans 1:16

HERE'S THE TEA.

We must ask ourselves, *What is the gospel*? You've definitely heard this word in church. Gospel most commonly translates to "good news." When looking at Scripture, we have to ask: Why would someone be ashamed of good news? You will find that submitting to the gospel will separate you from the ways of the world. The gospel demands we die to ourselves and allow Jesus to control our lives. And when we go against the current of this world, people will make fun of us. When we are ridiculed for something we believe, shame can creep in. But God's Word is the power of God. Once we understand the gospel is God's Word, the gospel *is* the power of God, and those who believe in it have salvation, we can finally move past shame completely. Once we begin to believe those things, we gain something extremely powerful: Confidence. Confidence is one of the most powerful tools we can have when living out the gospel in our own lives.

When we *know* God's Word is alive and active and has the power to save, there is no shame. Just confidence.

IF YOU WANT TO KNOW MORE
1 Cor. 1:18; 2:4; 4:20; 1 Thess. 1:5

1. Open your Bible and write out Romans 1:16.

2. If you were challenged to go outside and tell the first person you saw about Jesus, how would you feel and could you do it?

3. What is something you could do today to step out of your comfort zone to share the love of Christ?

TODAY'S FOCUS:

Confidence

It can be difficult to be confident in what we do. We don't want to come off as arrogant or full of ourselves. But putting confidence in the power of Scripture is necessary for personal and spiritual growth. **Be confident in what the Bible says. Be comfortable with not knowing everything, and know God will give us the confidence we need to fulfill His will.**

WATCH TODAY'S VIDEO

A 30-DAY DEVO CHALLENGE

SECTION 1

Day
FIVE

GEN Z VERSION

Take that noggin guard of savies and that big ol' knife of God's wordz.

Ephesians 6:17

ESV TRANSLATION

... and take the helmet of salvation, and the sword of the Spirit, which is the word of God. -Ephesians 6:17

HERE'S THE TEA.

Have you ever looked at a knight's armor? The armor itself could weigh up to 55 pounds![1] And to think people would fight in such heavy equipment. Your body would be exhausted, but the ultimate purpose is to protect yourself from harm. But what would a knight use to pierce the armor of his enemies? A sword. This is why the Bible describes itself as the "sword of the Spirit." In the armor of God, the sword is the only offensive weapon. Does that not give us an idea of just how truly powerful God's Word is? Scripture is capable of destroying the strongholds that seem impossible to get rid of. God hands us the only tool that can truly heal a heart stained with abuse or depression. God gives us what we need to fight back—to combat Satan as he actively tries to derail our pursuit of Christ. When Jesus was in the desert and Satan was trying to tempt Him, how did Jesus respond? He quoted Scripture. He gives us the tools to defend ourselves and others; tools that pierce through every lie, heartache, doubt, and temptation.

God's Word is a powerful sword, and it has been given to you. Will you pick it up?

IF YOU WANT TO KNOW MORE
1 Thess. 2:13; 2 Tim. 2:15; 1 Pet. 1:25

1. Open your Bible and write out Ephesians 6:17.

2. Describe the last time you picked up your sword (the Word of God) to fight a specific struggle you were dealing with.

3. In what way did God's Word help you with that struggle?

TODAY'S FOCUS:

Pick Up Your Sword

We all find ourselves in situations where we feel we are being attacked. And in those moments it can be easy to back down and choose not to fight back. But we must know that Satan is an enemy who never gives up and will attack us when we are the most vulnerable. **Choose today to see the Word of God as a weapon *and* as a requirement for your everyday arsenal.**

WATCH TODAY'S VIDEO

SECTION 1

Day
SIX

GEN Z VERSION

Moo moo food goes bye bye, and pedal pads take an L but God's scripts are perm.

Isaiah 40:8

ESV TRANSLATION

The grass withers, the flower fades, but the word of our God will stand forever.
                                        -Isaiah 40:8

HERE'S THE TEA.

Forever is a weird word. If you truly think about what the word *forever* means, it is impossible to fully comprehend. Yet we use it everyday in our conversations. We call people our "best friends forever." We exaggerate saying, "Man, I haven't seen that movie in forever!" And we use it to describe how long we will love people. But to be honest, almost nothing in our lives will last forever. Look around. What is one thing you see that you know will never fade away, break, or die? The largest trees in the world will one day fall, the most expensive mansions will be rubble, and even some of the stars we see will have died years ago. So much of what we value in this life will not last forever. So why put our trust and adoration into things that are temporary? Why devote so much of our time to things we don't love? Now, we aren't saying that what you do with your life is pointless or that there is no use in playing sports or getting a job.

But if everything we do isn't for the glory of the One who will be there after all of it is gone, then it's pointless. Christ tells us heaven and earth will pass away, but His words will *never* pass away.

IF YOU WANT TO KNOW MORE
Matt. 6:19-21; 24:35; 28:20; Heb. 13:5,8

A 30-DAY DEVO CHALLENGE

1. Open your Bible and write out Isaiah 40:8.

2. What is something in your past you believed would last forever that has now "faded"?

3. List three promises God has shown you through His Word.

TODAY'S FOCUS:

Forever

Don't miss out on what God is doing in you and in your family. Believe it or not, someone else's "forever" could be affected by your today. Only God and His Word will stand the test of time, so how will we choose to act on it? **Show God gratitude today for His everlasting words.**

WATCH TODAY'S VIDEO

SECTION 1

Day
SEVEN

GEN Z VERSION

Deep scrub 'em in the real talk, cuz your script is the real talk.

John 17:17

ESV TRANSLATION

Sanctify them in the truth; your word is truth.
-John 17:17

HERE'S THE TEA.

The truth is tricky. When we watch commercials and reality shows, it seems that the truth is hard to come by. This world has become so accustomed to lies that we have late night show games focused around them and we are taught that "little white lies" are nothing to worry about. So, how do we know what is truth and what is not? You can look at the evidence, but at the end of the day, so much is left up to trust. Trusting that someone is telling the truth is difficult when what they say seems unbelievable. When God tells us He will take care of us, it makes us feel good. But what happens when our lives are falling apart and we don't feel taken care of? Is it no longer truth because we feel this way? Do feelings have any part in deciphering truth? Our feelings and our circumstances are ever changing, but God's Word is constant. We have to be comfortable with questioning our own motives and preconceived ideas about the meaning and purpose of our lives. Seeking the truth is pivotal. We need to "sanctify," or "set apart" what is true.

When we seek Him, we will be set apart in His truth, discerning what's real from what's deceptive. Put your trust in Jesus and chase the truth.

IF YOU WANT TO KNOW MORE
Ps. 119:160; John 8:32; 6:13; 7:16-17; 2 Pet. 1:20

1. Open your Bible and write out John 17:17.

2. What things have you been taught that contradict God's Word?

3. Describe a time where your emotions took control over truth in your life.

4. Have you told yourself anything before that seemed right to you, but God's Word actually said something different than how you felt? Explain.

TODAY'S FOCUS:

Truth

When we step back and examine our emotions, we can tell a lot about ourselves: how we feel, what we value, and where we need guidance. However, it's important to remember that our emotions are only indicators; they don't tell the whole story. Sometimes we can be so overwhelmed with a particular negative emotion it's hard to recognize what is really true. Are you overwhelmed with sadness, confusion, disappointment, or anger? **Be honest with God about how you feel—He can handle it, and He will help you see what is really true about you, about Him, and about His love for you.** When we take our emotions to Him, He will help us see clearly.

WATCH TODAY'S VIDEO

A 30-DAY DEVO CHALLENGE

SECTION 1

Day
EIGHT

GEN Z VERSION

God bein' the real One, took us zombies and high key gave the real game.

Ephesians 2:4-5

ESV TRANSLATION

But God, being rich in mercy, because of the great love with which he loved us, even when we were dead in our trespasses, made us alive together with Christ—by grace you have been saved. -Ephesians 2:4-5

HERE'S THE TEA.

No one likes thinking about their sin. And as soon as we do, it's almost a reflex to stop before we get too upset. But taking an honest look at the sinful habits we've formed is essential to our growth. But why is sin even a big deal? Well, the Bible says "the wages of sin is death" (Rom. 6:23). Wages are what we earn, so by sinning we earn death. You may think that sounds unfair. But if you remember from Day 1, Jesus is the Word, and Jesus is God. And God created us, so for us to intentionally disobey has obvious consequences. Consequences being death. And so many of us are walking around dead. We disobey Him everyday. We ignore His commands and disrespect His plans for us on a daily basis. Yet, He loves us with such a passion that He was willing to do what it took for us to spend eternity with Him. We deserve nothing but death because of our sin, but because of Jesus giving everything up for *us*, we are now forgiven and alive in him.

We don't deserve life but the Word has given it to us.

IF YOU WANT TO KNOW MORE
Deut. 4:4; Ps. 56:13; 66:9; John 15:1-12

1. Open your Bible and write out Ephesians 2:4-5.

2. How would you define God's grace?

3. What are the attributes of a person who is "dead in (their) trespasses?"

4. What are the attributes of a person who is "made alive" in Christ?

TODAY'S FOCUS:

Alive in Christ

Take this time to pray, asking God to reveal any sin in your life that might be keeping you from being made fully alive in Christ.

Write out your prayer as you compare what it means to be "dead in your trespasses" versus being alive in Christ.

WATCH TODAY'S VIDEO

SECTION 1

Day
NINE

GEN Z VERSION

Dudes can't make it on sammie blankies alone, gotta feast on that real talk from God.

Matthew 4:4

ESV TRANSLATION

But he answered, "It is written,
'Man shall not live by bread alone, but
by every word that comes from the mouth
of God.'" - Matthew 4:4

HERE'S THE TEA.

What is the most hungry you have ever been? Have you ever gone so long without eating that it hurt? That is your spirit. Every one of us has a spirit that longs to be fed with God's words. But when the spirit goes hungry, we might not feel it like we would when our stomachs are craving food. When the Spirit is not being fed, we tend to slip away from where God wants us. We become more lazy and complacent. We welcome old sinful habits into our lives that we would normally run away from. Our human desires and feelings drive our actions and decision making. But our purpose on this earth is to glorify God. Just as you set time to eat every day and make it a priority, the same must be done for your spirit. We couldn't go a week without eating and not notice. So why do we starve ourselves spiritually for the same amount of time?

Once we begin to consistently feed on God's Word, we will notice it giving us more life every day.

IF YOU WANT TO KNOW MORE
Deut. 8:3; John 6:31-59; 1 Pet. 2:2; 1 Thess. 2:13

1. Open your Bible and write out Matthew 4:4.

2. How often are you reading Scripture to feed your soul? How could you make this a greater priority in your life?

3. What difference do you see in your everyday life when you are consistently in God's Word?

TODAY'S FOCUS:

Life Giving

We must hunger for God's Word just as we hunger for our next meal. Make it a habit just as you do with drinking water and eating lunch. Set a timer on your phone three times today to remind you to read today's verse. **Do everything you can to avoid letting your soul go hungry.**

WATCH TODAY'S VIDEO

A 30-DAY DEVO CHALLENGE

SECTION 1

Day
TEN

GEN Z VERSION

Your script is lit.
Psalm 119:105

ESV TRANSLATION

Your word is a lamp to my feet and a light to my path. -Psalm 119:105

HERE'S THE TEA.

Let's say you were given the task to follow a marked trail. If you can reach the end, you win a prize. It should only take a couple hours, the path is clearly marked, and you even have a map. Would you have trouble? Probably not, right? But what if it had to be done at night with no flashlights? Wouldn't the task be a lot more challenging? Of course. Without a source of light, any path would be difficult to follow. In this world, we are all on an uncertain path. It can often feel like we're lost on a mountain in the middle of the night with no help in sight. This is where God's Word comes in. His Word allows us to see where we are stepping. It is filled with reminders, stories we can learn from, and words of encouragement and discipline. God's Word lights up our paths of uncertainty. Now God may not show us the next ten steps or what the next day may look like, but He assures us He is there with every step we take.

No one knows the next steps to take or has a foolproof plan on how to succeed at life, but following and devoting yourself to God's Word will light your path.

IF YOU WANT TO KNOW MORE
Prov. 11:14; 16:9; Luke 1:79; John 16:13

1. Open your Bible and write out Psalm 119:105.

2. When was the last time you sought Scripture to give you clarity on a difficult decision?

3. How did Scripture show you how to deal with that situation?

TODAY'S FOCUS:

Guide

Today you will be faced with multiple choices. What do you want to eat for breakfast? Should you take an afternoon nap or binge watch Netflix? Will you react kindly to your parents or lash out in anger? Whatever the choices are, big or small, we can ask ourselves what is best for us. **Be aware of all the decisions you face today and ask yourself: Which of these choices will take me closer to being who God wants me to be?**

WATCH TODAY'S VIDEO

A 30-DAY DEVO CHALLENGE

SECTION 2: THE MINISTRY OF THE WORD

Day
ELEVEN

GEN Z VERSION

So Jesus spoke to the God squad, aka the chosies, aka the mana fam, "if you chill in the script, you're fam, and if ya know the real talk it'll drop the cuffs".

John 8:31-32

ESV TRANSLATION

So Jesus said to the Jews who had believed him, "If you abide in my word, you are truly my disciples, and you will know the truth, and the truth will set you free." -John 8:31-32

HERE'S THE TEA.

Jesus says the truth will set us free. Free from what? America is known as the "land of the free." Americans often claim they can do what they want because it is a "free country." So, what do people need freedom from? In this life, we know there are more than a few ways to feel guilty and blame ourselves for things that may or may not have been our fault. We become captives to our own selfish desires and, when we've gone too far down the wrong path, we feel helpless. Jesus tells us we are enslaved to our own sin. We become captive to what we allow into our lives and don't see how we will ever come out on the other side a better person. But in this passage, Jesus promises not only a way out, but also freedom from guilt, hatred, and shame. He promises us freedom. But on one condition: We must abide. Abide means to obey, stand by, uphold, and follow. We must abide in His words.

Freedom is being offered and all you have to do is accept it. Jesus paid your debt; He just asks that you trust Him.

IF YOU WANT TO KNOW MORE
Ps. 34:19; John 8:36; Gal. 5:1; 2 Cor. 3:17

1. Open your Bible and write out John 8:31-32.

2. Do you feel like you could be characterized as someone who "abides" in God's Word? Why or why not?

3. How is the truth found in God's Word different from the truth the world embraces?

TODAY'S FOCUS:

Freedom

In John 8:31-32, Jesus promises that if we "abide" in God's Word we will truly be one of His disciples. By abiding in His word, we also will *know* the truth, which will set us free.

Make a list of areas of your life where you are seeking freedom.

WATCH TODAY'S VIDEO

A 30-DAY DEVO CHALLENGE

SECTION 2

Day
TWELVE

GEN Z VERSION

I Marco polo-d God and He didn't leave me on read and snatched up all my scaries.

Psalm 34:4

ESV TRANSLATION

I sought the Lord, **and He answered me and delivered me from all my fears. -Psalm 34:4**

HERE'S THE TEA.

How often are we seeking something? I'm not talking about *Where's Waldo* or *I SPY* books. But in our normal, everyday lives: Are we seeking something? I know we are. We're all seeking something, whether it's attention and validation from friends, acceptance from parents, or love from anyone willing to offer it. But how often are we satisfied? How often do we actually find what we are looking for? It's normal to seek all of those things I mentioned, it's human nature. But these things can't cure what's going on inside of us. The Bible tells us we must seek God continually. If we seek Him, we will find Him. Jesus says we are guaranteed to find God if we just look. Think about that for a second. The moment we want to seek out God, the Creator of the universe, He will allow us to find Him. What is even more incredible is that God gave us Jesus to follow and study. By reading the Gospels we can know who Jesus was, what He did, and what He valued— we can receive guidance first hand.

Jesus made seeking the face of God more accessible and an actual possibility. So I ask, how often are you seeking something?

IF YOU WANT TO KNOW MORE
Ps. 24:3-6; 105:4; Jm. 5:10

1. Open your Bible and write out Psalm 34:4.

2. What does it mean to seek the Lord? What are some ways you can actively do this?

3. How much time in your day do you spend seeking the Lord compared to the time you spend on social media seeking others' attention? What is one step you could take toward changing your habits?

TODAY'S FOCUS:

Seek

In Psalm 46:10, God challenges us to "Be still, and know that I am God." **Under what circumstances do you take the time to give God your undivided attention?** Do you find yourself seeking God to address your wish list or do you seek God to better know His will?

WATCH TODAY'S VIDEO

A 30-DAY DEVO CHALLENGE

SECTION 2

Day
THIRTEEN

GEN Z VERSION

I Marco polo-d God and He didn't leave me on read and snatched up all my scaries.

Psalm 34:4

ESV TRANSLATION

*I sought the L*ORD*, and He answered me and delivered me from all my fears. - Psalm 34:4*

HERE'S THE TEA.

Have you heard the phrase "unanswered prayers"? People ask for something, then time passes, and they assume God doesn't want to give it to them. Later on, they are happy for that "unanswered prayer" because it would've been a bad idea in hindsight. But we must know there is no such thing as an unanswered prayer. Answers can be a no or a yes, but we must understand that God will always answer us. God already knows what we need before we ask (Matt. 6:8). He knows our needs, desires, and dreams. We ask, because asking develops trust. Romans mentions how the Spirit of God intercedes before us while we pray to Him (8:26-27). The Spirit is aware of our weakness and seeks the will of God through our communication to Him. Then God answers. He opens the door when we knock. We find Him when we seek. When we ask, it will be given to us (Matt. 7:7-8). If you believe these words, then what kind of prayers are you praying?

Knowing the Creator of the universe will answer your prayers, how will your prayers change? What will they look like?

IF YOU WANT TO KNOW MORE
Rom. 8:26-27,32-33; Jm. 5:10; 1 John 5:14-15

1. Open your Bible and write out Psalm 34:4.

2. Has God ever directly answered one of your prayers? What was the prayer and His answer?

3. When is the last time you prayed for God's will to be done, instead of Him giving you exactly what you wanted?

TODAY'S FOCUS:

God Answers Us

Do you find yourself frustrated by the fact that most days you have more questions than answers? We don't often receive the answers we want, or we don't get the answers at the moment we think we need them. God's timing is not our timing. Peace and contentment are found in seeking the Lord and in the knowledge that He answers us even when we do not necessarily hear Him. **Write down answers that you are seeking from the Lord today.**

WATCH TODAY'S VIDEO

A 30-DAY DEVO CHALLENGE

SECTION 2

Day
FOURTEEN

GEN Z VERSION

I Marco polo-d God and He didn't leave me on read, and snatched up all my scaries.

Psalm 34:4

ESV TRANSLATION

*I sought the L*ORD*, and He answered me and delivered me from all my fears. -Psalm 34:4*

HERE'S THE TEA.

When I think of the word *delivered*, I think of a package I ordered arriving on my doorstep. But this passage is talking about how God will deliver us from fear when we seek Him. This type of deliverance isn't a change of locations. God is talking about how He will remove the fear from inside us once we seek Him. That's something we might have a tough time comprehending. We often ask God to take us out of our current situation or stage of life. And when it doesn't happen, we become angry at God for not listening to us. But what if, instead of praying for a change of location, we actually prayed for a change of heart? If instead of praying for God to end the storm, we asked for enough strength and courage to endure it? Think of Shadrach, Meshach, and Abednego. They refused to bow to the false idol, even when threatened. They knew God *could* rescue them, but even if He didn't, they would still never bow. God chose to let them walk in the furnace, but He kept them safe. Their circumstances got increasingly more difficult but their hearts were delivered from fear.

Ask God to help you seek Him boldly, knowing He will deliver you.

IF YOU WANT TO KNOW MORE
Josh. 1:9; Ps. 34:17; Jm. 5:10; 1 John 4:4

1. Open your Bible and write out Psalm 34:4.

2. What are your three greatest fears in life?

3. In what ways have you sought the Lord to deliver you from those fears?

TODAY'S FOCUS:

Deliverance

If you knew God would deliver you from all your fears, how different would your life be? My bet is pretty different. We have a God who won't remove us from fearful situations but will remove the fear we feel. Isn't it comforting to know God will help us overcome anything we face as long as we trust Him? **Live confidently today, assured God will remove your fear.**

SECTION 2

Day
FIFTEEN

GEN Z VERSION

God's manual straight up slaps and CPRs my body brain.
Psalm 19:7

ESV TRANSLATION

The law of the Lord is perfect, reviving the soul; the testimony of the Lord is sure, making wise the simple. - Psalm 19:7

HERE'S THE TEA.

What is perfect? Can you name one thing you've seen or person you've met who is truly perfect? Obviously you can't. Perfection is impossible to find. Only one example of true perfection ever existed. Jesus. He was fully God and fully human. He came to seek and save the lost, help the sick, and give new life to those who are spiritually dead. And that takes us to the "reviving" part of the verse. Jesus, the Word, the law, is perfect and reviving to the soul. Every soul is dead before meeting Jesus. But just encountering the Son of Man once gives a breath of life to our soul. Not only does our soul receive new life, but we also now have a new energy and perspective. Just as someone who had a near death experience comes out with a new attitude of appreciation, we must be reborn and accept our new purpose. When our souls are revived, we draw closer to God and understanding His will for our lives as well as the need to reach others.

If we experience a new life and a revived soul, we can have the motivation and courage to share with others knowing they receive the same gift.

IF YOU WANT TO KNOW MORE
Ps. 19:8-11

1. Open your Bible and write out Psalm 19:7.

2. When you're feeling drained, what do you typically do to make yourself feel better?

3. What would your life look like if you believed God was able to give you new life everyday?

TODAY'S FOCUS:

Reviving

God's Word to your soul is like an energy drink or coffee to your body, without all the side effects. God uses His Word to bring your soul back to life. And even more than what those drinks can do, Scripture can bring us new purposes. **Focus today on how far God has brought you from who you used to be to the new creation you are now.** And if you haven't put your faith in Jesus yet, start today. Begin your new life as soon as possible.

WATCH TODAY'S VIDEO

A 30-DAY DEVO CHALLENGE

SECTION 2

Day
SIXTEEN

GEN Z VERSION

Don't flex on me, sus dude. If I slip, I don't dip. When life goes on dark mode, God keeps it lit.

Micah 7:8

ESV TRANSLATION

Rejoice not over me, O my enemy; when I fall, I shall rise; when I sit in darkness, the Lord will be a light to me. -Micah 7:8

HERE'S THE TEA.

We all experience darkness. We've all fallen and felt defeated and had moments when nothing in the world mattered to us because we felt forgotten. Unfortunately, there is no way to avoid such difficult times. But there is a big difference between falling and sitting in darkness with and without Christ. Without Christ, we have little motivation to fight and little to fight for. But with Christ, we have something more precious than gold: hope. You see, this verse says, even though I fall, I *will* rise; not maybe rise or "it's a possibility." He's telling us with certainty that God will bring us out of the pit of despair. He (Micah) knows his hope in God's salvation is the only thing that could possibly take him out of this darkness. Hope is not wishful thinking; it is a confident expectation. He says, "The Lord will be a light to me." Jesus as the way, the truth, and the life provides him a way out. Jesus is the one and only source for true Hope. Everything else just falls short.

There is no hope in death, but thankfully, we put our trust in the one Person who defeated death.

IF YOU WANT TO KNOW MORE
Isa. 38:18; Rom. 8: 24-25; 1 Pet. 1:13

1. Open your Bible and write out Micah 7:8.

2. Describe the last time you felt trapped in darkness.

3. How did God pull you out of that darkness?

TODAY'S FOCUS:

Hope

Hope is a beautiful thing. It gives us a glimpse into a better future. It allows us the opportunity to do better. It provides us the strength to get up with purpose each morning. Hope is a powerful thing, and because of Christ we now have it everywhere we go. **Challenge yourself to live in an attitude that values hope, and share that hope with at least one person today.**

WATCH TODAY'S VIDEO

SECTION 2

Day
SEVENTEEN

GEN Z VERSION

Chill vibes I full send. Not as the big blue sends. Don't let your chest thumper get triggered.

John 14:27

ESV TRANSLATION

Peace I leave with you; my peace I give to you. Not as the world gives do I give to you. Let not your hearts be troubled, neither let them be afraid. -John 14:27

HERE'S THE TEA.

When we think of peace, we think of harmony among people, no more fighting or wars. We think of those who seek inner peace through meditation, travel, and self-help books. Peace is discussed as something that we will achieve if we just work hard enough. Maybe if you do all the right things, then you'll find peace. I'm here to let you know that peace without Christ is unachievable. We can't accomplish lasting happiness without following God. Jesus gives us a peace that passes all understanding—it removes worry from this life and the next. With such peace comes an eternal security, an incomprehensible calming wave over your entire being. But how do we access such peace that we are not so overwhelmed by heartache, worry, or death? True peace can only be accessed by pursuing Jesus and His words.

Let go of your idea of peace and seek God's peace. He will give it to you. And the peace you will receive is only a glimpse into the incredible peace we will have while in eternity with Christ.

IF YOU WANT TO KNOW MORE
Gal. 5:22; Phil. 4:7; Col. 3:15; 1 Pet. 3:11; Rev. 21:4

1. Open your Bible and write out John 14:27.

2. How is peace we receive from people different from peace we receive from God?

3. What are you willing to give up to receive God's peace?

TODAY'S FOCUS:

Peace

Think of the last time you had peace. Was it a long time ago? When we pursue God, He will offer us peace even in the midst of a storm. **So today, don't focus on the chaos around you, but rather the overwhelming peace and strength God offers right in the middle of that chaos.**

WATCH TODAY'S VIDEO

A 30-DAY DEVO CHALLENGE

SECTION 2

Day
EIGHTEEN

GEN Z VERSION

Big props to you. You built me on fleek. Your moves are dope and my body brain knows it.

Psalm 139:14

ESV TRANSLATION

I praise you, for I am fearfully and wonderfully made. Wonderful are your works; my soul knows it very well.
-Psalm 139:14

HERE'S THE TEA.

You've probably seen this verse before on cards, Bible journals, jewelry, and even cheesy wooden signs in people's homes. It makes us feel good. And why wouldn't it? God loves us and created us to be a part of His plan. But David was focused on the actual physical body God gave him. It makes sense to be in awe of what God has created—the human body truly is incredible. For example, our noses can smell up to 1 trillion smells.[2] Taking one step uses over 200 muscles.[3] The detail our bodies possess is astounding, yet we take our bodies for granted. We don't think much of our bodies and even compare ourselves to others and think, "I wish I looked like that," or "Why did God give me *this* body?" While these are common thoughts, they are misleading—they lead us to place our identity in the wrong source. Our bodies should not define us but rather the God who created bodies in the first place. We are children of God, and His love for us goes beyond our physical appearance.

If we place our identity in Christ, then we become a new creation that goes beyond anything we could comprehend physically.

IF YOU WANT TO KNOW MORE
Rom. 15:17; 1 Cor. 6:17; 2 Cor. 5:17

1. Open your Bible and write out Psalm 139:14.

2. What do you like most about yourself? Take a moment and thank God for making you unique.

3. What are ways you can find your worth in Christ rather than your appearance?

TODAY'S FOCUS:

Identity

Challenge yourself today to focus on your heart rather than your appearance. Has Christ transformed you? Are you connected to Christ and finding your worth in Him? Write down five characteristics that described you *before* Christ and then five characteristics that describe you *now*.

WATCH TODAY'S VIDEO

SECTION 2

Day
NINETEEN

GEN Z VERSION

God hands out super smarties. His voice box brings the knows and gets.

Proverbs 2:6

ESV TRANSLATION

For the Lord gives wisdom; from his mouth come knowledge and understanding.
-Proverbs 2:6

HERE'S THE TEA.

Sadly, *wisdom* is not a word that intrigues us and leaves us wanting more. It almost seems like an old person word. Wisdom is what people with gray hair have. So why would we want it, right? Maybe we have the wrong idea of what wisdom means. So let's define it. James describes wisdom as pure, peaceable, gentle, open to reason, full of mercy and good fruits, impartial and sincere. Wisdom is knowing what to say and when to say it. Wisdom is knowing the right actions to take. Wisdom is knowing what future decisions will lead to our good and God's glory. Wisdom provides us with ways to help those who need it. Wisdom is crucial in the life of a Christian. Wisdom is for all ages and should never be looked down on. James tells us if we want wisdom, we just need to ask. God will give you wisdom through your daily reading and studying of His Word. God also places wise people in our lives who can help us make wise decisions and point us to Jesus.

Wisdom is a lot like the love God has for us: it's free to all who want it, and it never ends.

IF YOU WANT TO KNOW MORE
Prov. 1:7; 1 Cor. 1:30; Jm. 1:5; 3:13

1. Open your Bible and write out Proverbs 2:6.

2. Describe a time in your life you wish you would've had more wisdom.

3. Why is God's wisdom better than our knowledge?

TODAY'S FOCUS:

Wisdom

Today, focus on pursuing wisdom through God and through those who are older than you. Find one person you respect. Ask them for wisdom and advice on a specific situation you're facing and about any life lessons they can share with you.

WATCH TODAY'S VIDEO

SECTION 2

Day
TWENTY

GEN Z VERSION

He doctors your saddies and band-aids your boo boos.

Psalm 147:3

ESV TRANSLATION

He heals the brokenhearted and binds up their wounds. -Psalm 147:3

HERE'S THE TEA.

Some of the worst things someone can say when you're going through something traumatic or difficult are, "It could be worse," "everything happens for a reason," or "God won't give you anything you can't handle." People say such things because they see we are hurting and want to help. We want their words to heal us, but deep down we know they won't. As humans, we will encounter heartbreak and times of deep distress. We may believe getting out of bed is pointless and that things will never get better. Thankfully, we have someone who cares for us deeply. Jesus sees you and will be there for you when no one else will. Just because you think Jesus is silent or you can't feel His presence doesn't mean He isn't there. Jesus' sacrifice renews our spirits and forgives our sins. Jesus gave us the example that His body had to be broken for our souls to be made whole. He is the only One with the ability to heal our broken hearts and to actually understand what we are going through.

There is an enormous and unprecedented comfort that comes with knowing and following a God who loves you enough to care and empathize with everything you go through.

IF YOU WANT TO KNOW MORE
Ex. 23:25; Jer. 30:17; Mark 9:23; 1 Pet. 2:24

1. Open your Bible and write out Psalm 147:3.

2. What is something you want healing from?

3. Have you seen God heal others in your life? If so, how?

TODAY'S FOCUS:

Healing

No matter how broken the world is, Jesus can fix it. No matter how much the world hurts, Jesus can bring comfort. The God who conquers armies and destroys walls is the same God who can heal our broken hearts and mend the wounds of abuse. He loves you and is willing to meet you right where you are. He is bigger than whatever you are dealing with and will give you strength. **Today, pray for healing and focus on the times He has healed you in the past.**

WATCH TODAY'S VIDEO

SECTION 3: APPLYING GOD'S WORD

Day
TWENTY-ONE

GEN Z VERSION

Suit up. Don't play the bench, or you're straight up playing yourself.

James 1:22

ESV TRANSLATION

But be doers of the word, and not hearers only, deceiving yourselves. -James 1:22

HERE'S THE TEA.

Let's say someone came up to you and handed you a piece of paper that had directions for the cure for cancer. All you had to do was follow those directions. Would you do it? Would you follow those steps and help save countless lives? You'd have to be crazy not to right? Well here's another scenario. What if you were handed the tools to change people's lives and bring them peace? This scenario isn't so far-fetched. It's your reality. You have been handed a book that tells you how to turn your life around and find acceptance—and it changes the lives of the people around you, too. We have a cure for a sickness. Unfortunately so many of us are not doing our part in stopping this sickness. Christians are told to be doers of the Word; to hear the words of God and act on them. Do you realize the gospel has the power to change your eternal future and that of the people around you? It does. Don't keep it to yourself.

Our eternal destination is based on whether we hear God's words and respond accordingly. It may sound like a daunting task—that's because it is. But remember, if God is for us, who could possibly be against us (Rom. 8:31)?

IF YOU WANT TO KNOW MORE
Matt. 11:28-30; Titus 1:16; Jm. 2:18; 4:17

1. Open your Bible and write out James 1:22.

2. Why do you think we often listen but have a tough time following through?

3. How often do you read one of God's commands and put it off instead of acting on it immediately?

TODAY'S FOCUS:

Doer of the Word

The Bible is clear: We are saved by grace. We can do nothing to earn this salvation. But it doesn't end there. Jesus tells us we are His followers by listening and being doers of His Word. Because of the free salvation we have been given, we can follow through with living out His commands. **Today, choose one command the Word tells us and focus on it all day. Be a doer of the Word.**

WATCH TODAY'S VIDEO

SECTION 3

Day
TWENTY-TWO

GEN Z VERSION

Big grats to the dudes who stick to God's manual. Big grats to the dudes who listen up and telescope Him with your chest thumper.

Psalm 119:1-2

ESV TRANSLATION

Blessed are those whose way is blameless, who walk in the law of the Lord! Blessed are those who keep his testimonies, who seek him with their whole heart. -Psalm 119:1-2

HERE'S THE TEA.

It is often difficult to follow instructions. I mean, if I told you not to think about elephants, I know the first thing you pictured was an elephant. It's human nature to go against the guidelines we've been given. That's when it can become difficult, because Jesus gave us so many instructions to follow. And if we don't, there are consequences. But have you noticed that it's much easier to listen to rules from your best friend than from the principal at your school? The difference is the type of relationship. We are more likely to rebel against rules built purely on strict obedience and discipline than those built on love and mutual respect. We are far more likely to listen to and even obey those who know, love, and respect us. We obey God's Word not just because it contains His laws, but more importantly because its Author loves us. Once you love someone, you do what you can to please them and be faithful.

Jesus was always obedient to His Father. He literally showed us that loving God and obeying His commands go hand in hand.

IF YOU WANT TO KNOW MORE
Isa. 64:6; John 14:15,23

1. Open your Bible and write out Psalm 119:1-2.

2. When does it become most difficult to obey God's Word?

3. When God's Word goes against something you personally believe, how do you tend to react? How should you react?

4. Why is it difficult to obey God when we disagree with what He wants or says?

TODAY'S FOCUS:

Obedience

They say 99 percent obedience is still disobedience. It is easy to find yourself having the mindset of, "I'm a pretty good person. I listen to most of the rules and am better than most people, so I am good to go." But Jesus requires 100 percent obedience. We will fall and stumble in life, and that's where God's grace comes in, but we must not cut corners and compare ourselves to others. **Focus today on obeying your parents and God even in the smallest of ways.**

WATCH TODAY'S VIDEO

A 30-DAY DEVO CHALLENGE

SECTION 3

Day
TWENTY-THREE

GEN Z VERSION

My, dude, What is Gucci? What's God finna ask from you? Fair play, good deeds, and to walk the meek mile.

Micah 6:8

ESV TRANSLATION

He has told you, O man, what is good; and what does the Lord require of you but to do justice, and to love kindness, and to walk humbly with your God? -Micah 6:8

HERE'S THE TEA.

Some situations seem pretty black and white, but other times it is tough to tell right from wrong. This is why God has given us the Holy Spirit. The Holy Spirit is our helper, guiding us even in the toughest times. But even with help, we can sometimes be blinded by our own desires or swayed by our own ideas of what is right because it may benefit us. This passage tells us we are required to do justice—to hate evil and flee from wrong doing. At times, we will confidently choose to do the right thing, and God is proud in those moments. But we also know we will often choose the wrong and self-serving thing. Still, God shows us kindness. We don't deserve this grace. So what should we do when someone wrongs us? When someone mistreats us or makes a wrong choice, we have an opportunity to show them God's kindness. And when that kindness is received, it is our job to give thanks and stay humble.

Walking in humility is a sign that we understand we aren't the ones who give the gift of kindness. After all, it is Christ who is living in us.

IF YOU WANT TO KNOW MORE
Prov. 11:17; Rom. 7:14-20; Gal. 6:10; Col. 3:12

1. Open your Bible and write out Micah 6:8.

2. When is it most difficult for you to be kind?

3. What is the kindest thing that has ever been done for you? What happened, and how did it make you feel?

TODAY'S FOCUS:

Kindness

A common phrase people use when dealing with difficult people is "kill them with kindness." **Today, challenge yourself to spread kindness in a way where it brings life to you and your relationships.** Go out of your way to help someone. Do a handful of chores before being asked. Send someone an encouraging text. And pray that God would help you be a person who loves being kind.

WATCH TODAY'S VIDEO

A 30-DAY DEVO CHALLENGE

SECTION 3

Day
TWENTY-FOUR

GEN Z VERSION

Forklift your fam's saddies so God's sched is maxed out and relaxing all cool.

Galatians 6:2

ESV TRANSLATION

Bear one another's burdens, and so fulfill the law of Christ. -Galatians 6:2

HERE'S THE TEA.

You can't look on the news or social media without finding someone who needs help. We are constantly surrounded by people who are silently begging for help. Why wouldn't they just ask? Maybe some feel shame for reaching out. Some are under the illusion that they can handle it themselves. Some were raised to believe that asking for any type of help was a sign of weakness. Whatever the reason, even though everyone needs it, we often find it difficult to ask for help. And we make up plenty of reasons why we shouldn't help others. It's inconvenient. They can handle it on their own. Someone else will probably do it. They treated you poorly once. Whatever the excuse is, it's exactly that: an excuse. There are always a million reasons not to do something. But Jesus is very clear: We are here to serve and not to be served. He tells us to walk the extra mile; to give people more than they what they ask for.

So many people need our help, and God has equipped us to be the absolute best at helping. So let's stop waiting for them to ask us to pick up their burdens. Let's just start carrying them instead.

IF YOU WANT TO KNOW MORE
Prov. 3:5; Gal. 6:1-10

1. Open your Bible and write out Galatians 6:2.

2. What does it look like for you to carry the burdens of your friends and family?

3. Why is it important for us to help carry others' burdens?

4. When was the last time someone helped you carry a burden? What happened?

TODAY'S FOCUS:

Carry

We are given specific responsibilities to carry throughout our lives. With those come worry, stress, and anxiety. But we can give these cares to the Lord because He cares for us (1 Pet. 5:7). When worries begin to pile up, we often need help, so we must not be afraid to ask for help carrying our burdens. **Just as people help us, we must also seek opportunities to carry others' burdens. Watch for those people today and make sure you do what you can to help.**

WATCH TODAY'S VIDEO

A 30-DAY DEVO CHALLENGE

SECTION 3

Day
TWENTY-FIVE

GEN Z VERSION

Don't be a noob. Give your goodies cuz that's the stuff that gives God the smilies.

Hebrews 13:16

ESV TRANSLATION

Do not neglect to do good and to share what you have, for such sacrifices are pleasing to God. -Hebrews 13:16

HERE'S THE TEA.

What do you treasure most? Sleep? Relationships? Food? Sports? School? A hobby? After you've named it, ask yourself this: Would you be willing to give that up if it meant a loved one coming to Christ? This may seem dramatic, but it honestly might be a question you will face one day. The world God has given us is incredible. The freedom He allows us to chase our dreams and fulfill our passions is something we should be eternally grateful for. But just as God so freely gives us this life, He may at one point or another (or a thousand) ask us to put something on hold or give it up to benefit the kingdom. It may sound selfish to someone outside the faith—that our loving God would ask us to give up something we love so much, even for someone who treats us poorly. However, God was the first to give up something He loved for people who have continually treated Him poorly. We love others because God first loved us. We serve others because He served us.

We can still enjoy life, but when called to lay it down, we must sacrifice just as He did.

IF YOU WANT TO KNOW MORE
Acts 2:45; 20:35; 2 Cor. 9:7

1. Open your Bible and write out Hebrews 13:16.

2. What are three non-essential things you don't think you could live without?

3. What is something you would feel "uncomfortable" giving up for God?

TODAY'S FOCUS:

Sacrifice

Giving up anything we love can be difficult and make us feel incredibly uncomfortable. But as you've seen, Jesus asking us to give up our possessions or relationships is a possibility. **Focus on the things in your life today. If it came down to it, could you live without them?**

WATCH TODAY'S VIDEO

SECTION 3

Day
TWENTY-SIX

GEN Z VERSION

You're not getting in just cause you know the Big Man's name. Gotta do God's bidding to be the real ones.

Matthew 7:21

ESV TRANSLATION

"Not everyone who says to me, 'Lord, Lord,' will enter the kingdom of heaven, but the one who does the will of my Father who is in heaven." -Matthew 7:21

HERE'S THE TEA.

Imagine you go to church every week and never miss a Sunday. You volunteer and even teach when asked. You give generously and are always there to help. You are looked up to as an outstanding Christian in your community. And when you die, you stand face to face with Jesus. He looks at you to say, "I never knew you; depart from me." This will be the unfortunate reality for many. We can find ourselves so obsessed with our image and need for approval that we lose sight of our true purpose. Our desires and wants can distract us from our true purpose: doing God's will. We grow up being asked, "What are you going to do for the rest of your life?" We are subconsciously being told that this life is our own, but Christianity says the opposite. When we choose to follow Jesus, we are giving up the idea of having our own life. You give it up to accept a greater and better mission: to be dangerously generous, to forgive continuously, to love with no fear, and commit every fiber of your being to pursuing God's will in your life.

Denying yourself every day will not be easy but it will be worth it.

IF YOU WANT TO KNOW MORE
Jer. 29:11; Luke 9:23; Heb. 13:20-21

1. Open your Bible and write out Matthew 7:21.

2. How does your personal life plan compare to God's plan? What might need to change about your plans?

3. What things in your life would be difficult to give up if you knew God asked you to?

TODAY'S FOCUS:

God's Will

It's tough to imagine that God has a specific path and plan for each of us. But we must know God cares for every one of us deeply, and He wants us to live within His will for our lives. Sometimes that's a specific path like Jonah's, and sometimes it's as vague as, "follow Jesus and His teachings." **Pray and focus on what God is asking from you, and then ask yourself what you can do better to participate in His big plan.**

WATCH TODAY'S VIDEO

A 30-DAY DEVO CHALLENGE

SECTION 3

Day
TWENTY-SEVEN
GEN Z VERSION

Hang with me. I'll hang with you. The tree arms can't push berries if it ain't chillin with the plant rope, samesies with you peeps, unless you hang with me.

John 15:4

ESV TRANSLATION

Abide in me, and I in you. As the branch cannot bear fruit by itself, unless it abides in the vine, neither can you, unless you abide in me. -John 15:4

HERE'S THE TEA.

Receiving the Holy Spirit confirms that God abides in us. And if we choose to abide in Christ, then we will bear fruit. It is impossible for us to bear fruit if we are not abiding in Christ. It would be like plugging your phone charger into the outlet, not plugging in your phone, and expecting it to charge. Growth can't happen without being connected to the One who provides life. When we begin to abide in His words through daily prayer, worship, and studying, we will begin producing fruit in our lives. What does it look like to bear fruit? Galatians 5:22-23 says the fruit of the spirit are love, joy, peace, patience, kindness, goodness, faithfulness, gentleness, and self control. When we abide in Christ, these characteristics will naturally surface in us and will impact those who we come in contact with. "Fruit bearing" comes naturally because of our connection to Christ.

So pray that God reveals to you the fruit you are bearing and, more importantly, gives you the confidence you need to abide in Him whether you see the fruit or not.

IF YOU WANT TO KNOW MORE
John 15; Gal. 5:22-23; Col. 1:10

1. Open your Bible and write out John 15:4.

2. Read Galatians 5:22-23. Which fruit of the Spirit do you feel you are most lacking?

3. What three things can you do today to stay more connected to Christ?

TODAY'S FOCUS:

Bear Fruit

We know fruit can only be evident in our lives if we are staying connected to Jesus, and we can't have Jesus without the Word of God. After all, He *is* the word. So focus today on bearing fruit in your personal life. **Actively make the choice to stay connected to the Word today.** You might be surprised how quickly you bear fruit.

WATCH TODAY'S VIDEO

SECTION 3

Day
TWENTY-EIGHT

GEN Z VERSION

Listen up fam jam, hug it out with the sus dudes, be cool to the haters, be chill with those who roast you, and pray for those bully-bros.

Luke 6:27-28

ESV TRANSLATION

"But I say to you who hear, Love your enemies, do good to those who hate you, bless those who curse you, pray for those who abuse you." -Luke 6:27-28

HERE'S THE TEA.

We all have people who have wronged us. People who have honestly destroyed our spirits and treated us terribly. And this is one of the reasons following Jesus is tough, because we are not asked to love our enemies—we are commanded to love them. God doesn't give us recommendations that are totally optional. He commands us to love our enemies, do good to those who hate us, bless those who curse us, and pray for those who abuse us. Let's talk about that last one. Because getting down on your knees and truly praying for people who abuse you isn't easy. Are you willing to go before God and truly pray on their behalf? We have all fallen short of the glory of God. We all have sinned, and no one person is better than another. So who are we to deny someone the love of Christ and deprive them of the salvation He offers? While Jesus was dying on the cross, He was praying that God would forgive the people who were in the middle of murdering Him. What right do we have to refuse to love the difficult people in our lives?

Praying for those we hate or who hate us is not a suggestion but a command from Jesus Himself.

IF YOU WANT TO KNOW MORE
Mark 11:24; Rom. 12:12; Phil. 4:6-7; Col. 4:2

1. Open your Bible and write out Luke 6:27-28.

2. How often do you usually pray?

3. What can you do to make your prayer life more intentional and more of a habit?

TODAY'S FOCUS:

Prayer

Take the space below to write out your prayer for today. Make this prayer about other people who have treated you poorly. Ask God to transform your perspective. **Challenge yourself to look at those people as children of God who deserve forgiveness just as much as you.**

WATCH TODAY'S VIDEO

SECTION 3

Day
TWENTY-NINE

GEN Z VERSION

Hug it out, Fam cuz God hugged it out with you.

Ephesians 4:32

ESV TRANSLATION

Be kind to one another, tenderhearted, forgiving one another, as God in Christ forgave you. -Ephesians 4:32

HERE'S THE TEA.

Christianity doesn't always make sense. And maybe that's kind of the point. Jesus was on the cross asking God to forgive those who were killing Him. Stephen, while being murdered with stones, prayed that God wouldn't hold his attackers' sin against them. Peter literally turned his back on Jesus multiple times, and he became the rock upon which the church was built. The story of Jesus is surrounded with people who don't deserve to be forgiven but, for some incomprehensible reason, they are. And in this verse we are told to do the same. We are commanded to be kind and forgive everyone. And that doesn't make sense, right? *Everyone*? Jesus never told us this would all make sense. In fact, it is pretty clear it was never supposed to. As Christians we are called to question our own habits and thoughts to make sure we line up with God. And what He wants from us is to truly forgive everyone. We do that for one reason: because He forgave us when it didn't make sense.

That one terrible thing someone did to you, we've done that to Jesus every day. We must forgive because He forgave us first.

IF YOU WANT TO KNOW MORE
Luke 17: 3-4; Eph. 4:31-32; 1 John 1:9

1. Open your Bible and write out Ephesians 4:32.

2. Name one person you believe Christ is asking you to forgive right now.

3. What would it look like for you to forgive this person?

4. What is the most difficult part about forgiving others who have wronged you?

TODAY'S FOCUS:

Forgiving Others

Today's challenge is to forgive. Truly forgive the person whose name you wrote and ask God for help in moving on. **Ask God to throw away the grudge permanently and to help you be quick to forgive from now on.** It's tough, but you can do it through the power of the Holy Spirit.

WATCH TODAY'S VIDEO

A 30-DAY DEVO CHALLENGE

SECTION 3

Day
THIRTY

GEN Z VERSION

I took you to class, y'all got the homework— now gas up that project, and God, the CEO of all chill vibes, will be fam forever.

Philippians 4:9

ESV TRANSLATION

What you have learned and received and heard and seen in me—practice these things, and the God of peace will be with you.
-Philippians 4:9

HERE'S THE TEA.

We have had the Bible for as long as we've been alive. It's on our phones and more accessible than ever. The answer to heartache, love, guilt, pride, and every other struggle we might have lies within those words. It's the most captivating and life-altering piece of literature we will ever find. Its more than catchy one-liners and motivation for your next tattoo. It is literally the Word of God. The Creator of every human being, the universe, and everything we will ever know has made His words available to us. He has promised us a life of joy, peace, wisdom, and unconditional love. He has told us exactly what to do to receive an eternal life of no hurt, no pain, and no death. He has given us His only Son so we could be with Him forever. He's done all of this through His Word. Now the question is: What will you do about it? You've heard the gospel, and you understand what is at stake. Now it's time to respond.

You have the gift of salvation, now go. Go abide in Him. Love others as He loved us. Make disciples. Pray to your Father in heaven. Obey the Word. Change the world.

IF YOU WANT TO KNOW MORE
Luke 8:21; John 13:17; Rom. 2:13

1. Open your Bible and write out Philippians 4:9.

2. What is the most difficult part about putting what you've learned into practice?

3. What three things will you start doing today to make the Word of God a priority in your life?

TODAY'S FOCUS:

Practice

In every situation, we face a dilemma. Will we or will we not glorify and obey Christ? With every word we say and every conversation, we have to ask ourselves that question. It may seem difficult to remember and act on that in every circumstance, but just like anything else, the more we practice the better we get. **Be intentional about choosing to follow Christ with your actions today.**

WATCH TODAY'S VIDEO

𝔚𝔥𝔞𝔱'𝔰 𝔑𝔢𝔵𝔱

You did it. You spent 30 days with us in this devotional. They say it can take doing something consistently for at least 66 days to form a new habit.[4] It sounds like you're off to a great start in making the study of God's Word a priority in your life.

As Christians, our main goal is to listen to what God has told us to do. He has told us to stay connected to Him, and one of that most important ways to abide in Him is through devotion to His words. We hope you've learned that. We hope you've discovered the absolute need for God's Word in your life. That Scripture isn't a nice suggestion or a how-to guide for Christianity, but it's an absolute necessity to our way of life. We pray you stay committed to diving into God's Word each day as you move forward. That the sun will not go down before you have had the privilege to study this Book He has given to us.

So thank you for reading this, thank you for listening to God's calling. And always remember to stay salty and lit, fam.

Matthew 5:13-16

SOURCES
1. Mark Cartwright, "The Armour of an English Medieval Knight," Ancient History Encyclopedia, June 13, 2018, https://www.ancient.eu/article/1244/the-armour-of-an-english-medieval-knight/.
2. Joseph Stromberg, "The Human Nose Can Distinguish Between One Trillion Different Smells," SMITHSONIANMAG.COM, Smithsonian Magazine, March 20, 2014, https://www.smithsonianmag.com/science-nature/human-nose-can-distinguish-between-one-trillion-different-smells-180950175/.
3. Xavia Malcolm, "How many muscles do we use take a single step forward?", Health Beat, Jamaica Hospital Medical Center, March 16, 2015, http://jamaicahospital.org/newsletter/how-many-muscles-do-we-use-take-a-single-step-forward/.
4. Gretchen Rubin, "Stop Expecting to Change Your Habit in 21 Days," Psychology Today, October 21, 2009, https://www.psychologytoday.com/us/blog/the-happiness-project/200910/stop-expecting-change-your-habit-in-21-days.